In the Waiting

A DEVOTIONAL

AC Sarreal

TRILOGY CHRISTIAN PUBLISHERS
Tustin, CA

TRILOGY

Trilogy Christian Publishers
A Wholly Owned Subsidiary of Trinity Broadcasting Network
2442 Michelle Drive
Tustin, CA 92780

In the Waiting • A Devotional

Copyright © 2025 by AC Sarreal

Scripture quotations marked CSB are taken from the Christian Standard Bible®, Copyright © 2017 by Holman Bible Publishers. Used by permission. Christian Standard Bible, and CSB®, are federally registered trademarks of Holman Bible Publishers.

Scripture quotations marked ASV are taken from the American Standard Version of the Bible. Public domain.

Scripture quotations marked NIV are taken from the Holy Bible, New International Version®, NIV®. Copyright © 1973, 1978, 1984, 2011 by Biblica, Inc.™ Used by permission of Zondervan. All rights reserved worldwide. www.zondervan.com. The "NIV" and "New International Version" are trademarks registered in the United States Patent and Trademark Office by Biblica, Inc.™

Scripture quotations marked BLB are taken from the Berean Literal Bible. Public domain.

Scripture quotations marked ESV are taken from the ESV® Bible (The Holy Bible, English Standard Version®), copyright © 2001 by Crossway Bibles, a publishing ministry of Good News Publishers. Used by permission. All rights reserved.

Scripture quotations marked NLT are taken from the Holy Bible, New Living Translation, copyright © 1996, 2004, 2015 by Tyndale House Foundation. Used by permission of Tyndale House Publishers, Inc., Carol Stream, Illinois 60188. All rights reserved.

Scripture quotations marked NASB are taken from the New American Standard Bible® (NASB), Copyright © 1960, 1962, 1963, 1968, 1971, 1972, 1973, 1975, 1977, 1995 by The Lockman Foundation. Used by permission. www.Lockman.org.

Scripture quotations marked KJV are taken from the King James Version of the Bible. Public domain.

For information, address Trilogy Christian Publishing Rights Department, 2442 Michelle Drive, Tustin, CA 92780.

Trilogy Christian Publishing/ TBN and colophon are trademarks of Trinity Broadcasting Network.

For information about special discounts for bulk purchases, please contact Trilogy Christian Publishing.

Manufactured in the United States of America

Trilogy Disclaimer: The views and content expressed in this book are those of the author and may not necessarily reflect the views and doctrine of Trilogy Christian Publishing or the Trinity Broadcasting Network.

10 9 8 7 6 5 4 3 2 1

Library of Congress Cataloging-in-Publication Data is available.

ISBN: 979-8-89597-196-3

ISBN: 979-8-89597-197-0 (ebook)

This God inspired work is dedicated to my spouse, who has continuously been there to support my dreams.

Preface

But they that wait upon the LORD shall renew their strength (Isaiah 40:31, KJV)

A 21-day devotional dedicated to waiting on the LORD.

Contents

Day 1. Wait 1

Day 2. Waiting in Prayer 4

Day 3. The Motives of Our Heart 6

Day 4. Fasting 9

Day 5. Waiting and Worship 12

Day 6. El Roi 15

Day 7. Waiting is Preparation 18

Day 8. One to Another 21

Day 9. Absence Makes the Heart Grow Fonder 24

Day 10. Experience the Supernatural 27

Day 11. Filled With the Holy Spirit 30

Day 12. The Fruit of the Spirit..................................... 33

Day 13. Love 36

Day 14. Joy 39

Day 15. Peace 42

Day 16. Patience 45

Day 17. Kindness 48

Day 18. Goodness 51

Day 19. Faithfulness 54

Day 20. Gentleness 57

Day 21. Self-Control 60

DAY 1

Wait

Waiting is hard. Whether it's sitting in a waiting room for the doctor's news, a test result, or for the server to bring the bread and appetizers; waiting is hard! When I committed to become a dedicated, Spirit filled Christian my first thought was, *what in the world does it mean to 'wait on the LORD'?!* In times of trouble, we have all heard our loved ones, friends, or our pastor tell us to wait on the LORD. Chances are, if you are reading this devotional, you are in a period of waiting.

> *This reminds us to wait on the LORD; Be of good courage, and He shall strengthen thine heart. Wait, I say, on the LORD.* (Psalms 27:14, KJV)

Do we often conduct ourselves in a productive or God-honoring way when we wait? Or are we like little children who forgot to use the potty before we left the house and now we are in the middle of the 5 freeway at 5 p.m. and you "have to go!"?

Today is about seeking the Holy Spirit's guidance and wisdom in understanding why and how we should wait. Today is less about reading a ton of scripture, and more about allowing the Holy Spirit to inspire you. This is the foundation of creating an even deeper relationship with God.

Focusing on what God is providing in the waiting and what God is providing as a result of waiting on Him can help us. We are strengthened by God, and we should be strong. He doesn't tell us to be weary or be angry. In fact, He doesn't even reference emotions in that psalm. He says to be strong. Our first instinct in waiting is to be anxious, or sad, or angry. There's a reason the vernacular "hangry" was created because waiting for food can elicit some interesting behavior even in the best Christian models. God knew what He was doing when He called us to fast and tame our flesh (we will discuss this further in the near future).

So many emotions can flood us in the waiting but God gives us a declaration that doesn't have to do with feeling. It has to do with character and being. Being strong and of good courage. Sounds simple but, as you know, it is far from easy to do. We can only do and be those things if we practice God's word and allow the Holy Spirit to sustain us. Will you allow God to sustain you during this time of waiting? Can you focus your mind on Jesus and what He has sacrificed for you? Do you trust God to meet your needs during this time and all others?

Father, You are good and merciful. As I walk out my day, in the waiting, I pray that Holy Spirit would provide all that I need. May I receive the strength in facing my current situation. May You provide peace that surpasses all understanding. I trust in You God and know You are here with me. May this time of waiting on You strengthen my heart and my relationship with You. I pray for Your edification and look forward with joy and hope to what is to come. In Jesus's name I pray. Amen.

DAY 2

Waiting in Prayer

King David was confined to a cave. Waiting on the Lord is easier when you don't have much else to do. He was so distraught in the cave that he was literally crying out to the Lord. He had constant dialogue with God. Lament, sadness, despair. Although despite all of his groanings to God, David continued to trust and know that God was with him.

Sometimes, we too, feel backed into a corner. Do you ever find that you have something you are waiting on to the point where it occupies every part of your mind and day? That is a good indicator that you should be spending time in prayer.

Dwell. It's an interesting word. Dwell can also mean abide, lodge, stay, inhabit, reside or even in some instances of the Bible it can mean to establish permanently. God reminds us to dwell. Psalms 23:6 might be the most popular scripture where "dwell" is used. As it goes, ... and *I will dwell in the house of the Lord forever.* (Psalms 23:6, KJV)

God wants us to dwell with Him. Not to dwell on our problems or troubles. Troubles will come and go, but God will never depart from those who love Him. We should focus on our prayer time being an intimate time with God. If we allow Holy Spirit to truly dwell within us and have that confidence that we can encounter Him in the secret place it can help us through times of waiting.

He who dwells in the shelter of the Most High will abide in the shadow of the Almighty. (Psalms 91:1, ESV)

So go into your prayer closet, or your secret place, and spend time with the One who is our refuge and fortress while you wait. In the waiting we can be edified and Holy Spirit may have an opening to minister to us in our time of need.

Father, I trust in You and I thank You for being my shelter. I know that You are the one who can provide us refuge and shield us even from ourselves and our own emotions. I pray that You continue to make Yourself known to me in the secret place as I seek You out. May I never grow weary of spending time with You especially in times when I need You most. Help me to focus on Your will. I know that if I continue to press into the ministering of the Holy Spirit, He will reveal truth and wisdom for all that I need at this moment. Glory to You, God, as I expectantly await Your deliverance! In Your name, Amen.

DAY 3

The Motives of Our Heart

Why does God make us wait? Seems like a simply loaded question. Waiting can reveal the true nature of a person. Just look at how someone might act if they don't have internet service and they are in the middle of watching or listening to something online. Do they panic? Do they try to fix it? Do they just sit and wait for it to resolve itself? I've seen the good, the bad and the ugly when the internet "goes down."

On the flip side, what if we received everything we asked for? What if we always got what we wanted right away?

I thank God every day that I don't get most of the things I have asked for in my forty plus years on earth. I would have ended up with a home that would be at the bottom of the sea right now, too many pets that I can't care for, and a person that I could not see myself being married to in this present day and age. God has saved me from a lot of things I wanted, but were not good for me. God always knows what is best.

I am always thankful that my sinful nature, my instinct to act on my emotions or just accidental/negligent actions cannot change or thwart God's will. Take great encouragement that God's timing is perfect, even when we are not obedient to follow His leading.

Recommended Reading - Exodus 14

The Lord will fight for you; you need only to be still.
(Exodus 14:14, NIV)

While we wait on the Lord, we shouldn't be running around like a chicken with our head cut off. Chaos does not come from God. Chaos is evidence of the enemy. What an amazing thought to know that we don't need to swing our swords and throw axes in order to win battles. The battle belongs to the Lord. We can be still in the natural but in the spiritual we know the Lord is winning battles on our behalf. Are you willing to trust that God will help you? Are you willing to take a leap of faith even when things look like they are impossible? Maybe, just maybe in the waiting God is looking to see if your spiritual connection to Him is as important in being restored or set up as your internet is. We have to be more than just waiting. Why not take advantage of our direct line to God and use that connection to spend as much time with Him as we possibly can. One thing the enemy really hates is when we spend time with God. So, the next time you have the opportunity to wait on the Lord, don't just turn on the television or browse social media. Get down on your knees and spend time with the Father.

Father, I look up toward You during times of waiting so that I may know You better. Please keep me hungry for Your presence while I wait on You. Rather than be busy or distracted, help me to continue to pursue You and Your wisdom. The enemy will try to turn me away with entertainment and other interesting things, and today I say, 'NO' to those things. I want to be connected to You as much as possible so that I can discern and know Your voice when You instruct me. I look forward to this battle being won, and for You to be glorified in Jesus's name.

DAY 4

Fasting

Oh no. Yes, I said it. Fasting! Dun dun duuuun. For someone like myself, who has grown up in a family where life revolves around food, the word "fasting" can bring out a pretty strong emotion. Might I go as far as to say I used to be offended if someone even suggested I fast. How dare they tell me to starve myself! I am not about to die... and yet here I am alive and well.

I have made it through a handful of serious fasts and many little ones. I have only been fasting for a number of years but I have noticed that there has been an acceleration of things from God since I began to implement fasting in my life. Jesus didn't say, "If you fast..." He said "WHEN you fast...". This obviously is an expectation. There is nothing more productive in taming the flesh than taking away the basic necessity of food. An amazing reflection of self and your true colors are seen when you are feeling deprived of something that is meant to sustain your life. If you haven't gotten to a point where God is your everything, then fasting will certainly bring you to that realization when you come out alive and well at the end of it. In fact, many can argue that despite not having any nutrients you can feel wonderful during a fast when done correctly.

The key component that is paramount when fasting is to pray. If you don't pray on a fast, it's just a diet. There is no breakthrough, reflection or glory to God if your prayer life isn't hand in hand with your fast. Seek God's heart and it is only when you become so desperate and starving for earthly nourishment can you finally turn to the Father and truly know that He is the only true food that you need. Fasting and praying reveals how much earthly things fall short of satisfying us when we experience true feeding from the Father.

If you are waiting for a breakthrough, fasting can help keep your mind on God and what He wants from you during the waiting. During your fasting, pray and ask Him what you are to learn in this season. What is it that He is teaching you? Fasting will quickly put in perspective who or what we truly serve. A wise person once said, "Don't give up your blessing for a cupcake!" Or you can insert whatever food/craving you have in that statement. If you feel like you've been waiting for a long time, perhaps fasting and prayer is what is in order.

> [29] *Once when Jacob was cooking some stew, Esau came in from the open country, famished.* [30] *He*

said to Jacob, "Quick, let me have some of that red stew! I'm famished!" (That is why he was also called Edom.)[31] Jacob replied, "First sell me your birthright."[32] "Look, I am about to die," Esau said. "What good is the birthright to me?"[33] But Jacob said, "Swear to me first." So he swore an oath to him, selling his birthright to Jacob.[34]

Genesis 25:29-34 (NIV)

Father, You are worthy of all I can give and all I can do. Help me to learn to seek You above all earthly things. Strengthen me and help me commit to a fasted prayer life. In my waiting, I will continue to find ways to grow closer to You and know that fasting will allow me a deeper relationship with You. I recognize that it is something that Jesus did and so I should commit to doing the same. I look forward to experiencing a connection with You that is unique and different so as to know You even better. I also wait on Your prompting of how and when I should fast and pray so that I may be obedient in all that You call me to do. I wait with joyful expectation of the breakthrough and blessing before me. In Jesus's name.

DAY 5

Waiting and Worship

Dance like nobody's watching. I'm sure we have all heard that phrase before. What if we danced like God was watching? Would our worship be different? I believe so.

When my kids were really young, they would ask me to stop what I was doing so I could see them twirl, or do a cartwheel, or jump off the couch. It was such a small thing but they wanted me to be captivated by them. They wanted that small moment of uninterrupted time to show me what they could do.

What if we sought after God in that way? What if we sought after His favor so much that we danced like He was watching? How different our worship would be. Especially when waiting on the Lord, we want God's attention. We want to know that Jesus sees us. Perhaps, we should take a page from the youth and become like little children after our Father's special attention. Maybe we only twirl, or have one moment of raising a Hallelujah, but recognize that the Father sees it. We should dance before God just as David did. He is worthy of our praise and we can keep things in perspective in the waiting when we remember this about all He has done for us.

> *It was before the Lord, who chose me rather than your father or anyone from his house when he appointed me ruler over the Lord's people Israel—I will celebrate before the Lord. ²² I will become even more undignified than this, and I will be humiliated in my own eyes. But by these slave girls you spoke of, I will be held in honor.*
>
> 2 Samuel 6:21-22 (NIV)

More to Read: 2 Samuel 6:14-22

If you are waiting for a breakthrough, or an answer to prayer, look to heaven and cry out to God. Sing to God at the top of your lungs, and cry out shouts of praise to Him. Show God your heart is for Him, and "Dance like He is watching."

God, may I have bold worship before You. You are so worthy of it all. Everything You have done for me is truly worthy of Your glory. My worship in my most fervent and exuberant ways still pale in comparison to who You are. You deserve all I can possibly give and more. I pray that my worship would be acceptable to You. That You would turn Your face toward me for even just a moment in my time of waiting and watching in expectant joy of what You will do in my life. May my fear of man dissipate, and may my gratefulness grow and be demonstrated to You in every circumstance regardless of my environment. Bless our time together in my connecting and worship of You. In Jesus's name.

DAY 6

El Roi

Are You there God? I went through a season where I felt like I was doing and doing and doing just to figure out where God wanted to place me. I didn't recognize my call yet and while I was waiting to hear from God, I kept looking for places to serve and put myself. Sometimes, in the waiting, we are moving forward without God, and that can build up resentment or even feelings of not being appreciated. I fell into that trap myself.

When Hagar was running from Sarah and the angel of the LORD approached her and spoke with her, she knew she was seen. What an amazing testament to God's goodness. Not only was Hagar seen during a time of turmoil, but God revealed Himself and spoke directly to her. She knew in that moment that she was truly seen by God. When we recognize that God sees us, that He is El-Roi, then the waiting is much more bearable.

> [13] *She gave this name to the LORD who spoke to her: "You are the God who sees me," for she said, "I have*

now seen the One who sees me. (Genesis 16:13, NIV)

When I felt the resentment of doing without being acknowledged I felt miserable. There was a moment while I waited on God to reveal to me why I felt this way. One thing He reminded me of was that I prayed for something very specific and that exact same day I got confirmation that God had answered that prayer. It was an "Aha!" moment and I immediately told a close friend that God reminded me that He always answers my prayers and that it didn't matter whether people recognized me or not because God sees me! Right as the words came out of my mouth and I declared the truth of God I suddenly was met with someone thanking me for a project I had done. I also began throughout the day having people saying "great job" or "thank you" for helping or serving in something. I was able to break that bond of selfishness and resentment in just remembering that God sees me. He is, in fact, El Roi. I no longer felt I was spinning my wheels doing and doing for nothing and without result. It certainly helped me in waiting for what God was really trying to show me.

When you are in the desert and looking for water or some life to come back to you, remember to turn to God. Cry out to Him and acknowledge Him in your waiting. He sees you.

Thank You, Father, for Your revelation. Thank You that You are ever present in my life, and despite the fact that I am miniscule in this universe You not only SEE me but You care deeply for me as an individual, and as Your child. Thank You for the gentle correction in the moments that I am waiting for a breakthrough or understanding. May I always remember that the waiting is for me to be edified and to be drawn closer to You. Help me to see You in everything just as You see me. Help me to see myself the way You see me. In Jesus's Holy name.

DAY 7

Waiting is Preparation

Read Luke 12:35-40

When in the waiting, sometimes you can get stuck in no action or move too fast in presumption. That's why paying close attention to Holy Spirit is so important. Imagine that your friend is trying to tell you something very important but you're so far away that you can't hear them over the noise of the street or people talking or music playing or other media being in your way. You want a captive audience with Holy Spirit. Be so close that He can whisper in your ear uninterrupted even when there is noise all around you.

Being astute to Holy Spirit's prompting, we can be led astray when we don't focus intentionally on what the Holy Spirit is conveying or speaking to us. Proximity is so important. Can you feel the presence of God? If you can't recognize God's presence in everyday life then the waiting will definitely be far more challenging.

I have always loved to fish and as a child I was quite good at it. At times, I would even catch the most fish compared to my older and wiser counterparts (i.e. fishing buddies). At five years old, God had given me the gift of patience. Being out on the river I remember my uncle often reminding me to be very still and very quiet so that we wouldn't scare the fish away. I wanted so badly to catch something that I would hold very still. So still that you can hear a leaf slowly fall onto the water. Imagine now, that the quietness of the leaf falling into the water is like the Holy Spirit speaking to us. You better be really still and really focused to hear it. I would urge you to practice and remember what that leaf touching the water sounds like, and then in your quiet time with God use the same level of focus to listen to Him.

Once you learn to hear the still small voice don't stop there. Put that thought, message, idea, vision into action. God is preparing us while we wait and when the waiting time is over only you yourself will know if you did everything God asked of you. Will you be prepared for the answer or for the breakthrough? Waiting has its purpose and we should welcome the time that God is allowing to forge us for His next instruction for you.

God, I thank You for times of waiting. Your mercy is so prevalent in the wilderness when You are building me into the person You have called me to be. I look to You always for guid-

ance and know that I must pay attention to Your promptings in order to take action when the time comes. In the meantime, please continue to speak to me through Holy Spirit that I can be prepared for what is to come and to execute my appointment from You with excellence. You are my wonderful counselor, and my almighty Savior. I continue to fix my eyes on You, Jesus.

DAY 8

One to Another

Many hands make for light work. Can I tell you that much sharing can also make for light work of the mind, or in other words less stress and burden? God blessed us with community. There is a reason that God put a strong emphasis in Ekklesia. The body is meant to be in union and as one. If we can't carry our own burdens, then we are to give it to God. If God brings a group of other God loving individuals to help with your anxieties, stresses or to lift you up you should receive it as there is healing when we as the body of Christ work together as one.

> *Everyone should look out not only for his own interests, but also for the interests of others.* – (Philippians 2:4, CSB)

> *Therefore encourage one another and build each other up as you are already doing.* – (1 Thessalonians 5:11, NLT)

Carry one another's burdens; in this way you will fulfill the law of Christ. – (Galatians 6:2, ASV)

My family is notorious for keeping secrets. Growing up we suffered from a spirit of gossiping. Oddly enough, the devil was able to twist something that was ultimately good and turn it into something that was no longer glorifying God. If someone knew something about a family member (i.e. someone was sick, someone had an unfortunate circumstance, or an unexpected pregnancy) they would pass it through the gossip train. Supposedly, no one was supposed to know but everyone knew eventually. What my family didn't pick up on was that the gossip wasn't gossip if it was a prayer request. If only they took what they knew and prayed into it or at least shared it with the right perspective in mind. Not the type of perspective that makes you shame someone but with the perspective that your heart is in the right place and you want to lift said person in prayer. That is what one to another is meant to be like, not some direct connection to Hotline Hector who served no purpose but to know someone's business.

In this day and age, I know we could all learn to share and be open with those we trust in the body of Christ. We are meant to lift each other up and give each other encouraging words. Those words should be stemming from the Holy Spirit and welling up inside of you. So, if you are so full of the Holy Spirit and you get hit with a gossip stick then only goodness and prayer should spill out.

Lord, I praise You for Your patience with me, unlike my tendency to be impatient with You. May I remember that You provide us with support and love. I need only recognize through Your Holy Spirit when and in what form it takes. I receive it as You bring these life rafts into my path. I pray for continued hope as I await Your help and purpose for me in the waiting. Help us all to be ever vigilant in what You have to offer and provide every day of our life. You are our daily bread. Thank You from this contrite and grateful heart. In Jesus's name.

DAY 9

Absence Makes the Heart Grow Fonder

I once had a tennis coach in high school who used to ask the question: "Does absence make the heart grow fonder? Or is it, out of sight; out of mind for you?" Odd for teenagers to be approached this way whilst running the bleachers. I only realized later in life that he was asking about our own personal convictions and what our natural tendency was. He was planting a seed. I also found out a decade later that he was a pastor of his own small church just down the street from where I lived. What a blessing it was to have a man of God influencing young people albeit covertly out on the playing field.

Speaking of the heart growing fonder; in the waiting we have the opportunity to keep pressing in toward God or to give up and turn away from God. Perhaps if you've been a believer for a long time, you might ask yourself, *How could I possibly turn away from God?* I might suggest that even giving up on the idea that God can fix a specific problem, or answer the question you are waiting for is in a way turning away from God, and turning your head toward a person or even turning to yourself. Even a man after God's own heart (i.e. David) got too relaxed and stopped waiting upon the Lord. The fact that he stopped listening to God and stopped going out to battle in the spring when kings go off to war, sent David on a chain reaction of events that would destroy a part of his life. It happens to the best of us.

Further suggested reading: 2 Samuel 11 and 12.

We should long for God so much that we can't wait to get an answer. In fact, waiting should bring a level of excitement. When I wait on the Lord for something and truly am expecting Him to deliver a blessing, a promise, or an answer to prayer, I am so excited that I can't contain my joy. Yes, I admit I am the person who is annoyingly joyful in the most inappropriate times. Sorry, not sorry.

I finally understood why people love Hallmark movies where the guy gets the girl and all is well with the world. The feeling of falling in love, or expecting a proposal, or seeing the happy ending is a naturally joyful feeling. Why? When we fast and pray and wait on God, we get that same feeling of expectant joy but in greater amounts. If we are obedient and do things God's way, absence does make the heart grow fonder. Do we long for God the way we long for a big date to start? For a returning soldier to come home? For your children to open their Christmas gifts? There are many moments in my life that feel that way, and being expectant for God to move makes all those other moments pale in comparison to His answer. I pray you find that same expectant joy and excitement, that your heart grows fonder for Him whose banner over you is love.

God, I look expectantly toward You. I pray and desire a greater connection. May I long for You more than the way I long for the things of this world for I recognize that they are temporary. You are forever and You carry me in Your loving hands. I pray that my joy and hope is increased in this time of waiting and that I get to experience or encounter You in a deeper way. You are my rock and I can't wait to see what is next for me. I pray that Your banner of love stays over me all the days of my life. In Christ's holy name.

DAY 10

Experience the Supernatural

Now that we are all prayed up and we have been on this journey for the last week and a half I am praying that you would find your greater vision and your spiritual eyes would be opened to the supernatural things that God has planned in the waiting. There is always something God is working on behind the scenes. Unless we stop to reflect on the blessings that happen even in the midst of chaos, we can't appreciate the way God is working for the good of those who love Him. Do you believe He is at work for your sake? If and when you do actually believe that He is, then you will be able to have the right posture of your heart. When your heart is right with God, then will you be able to see, or at least get a glimpse of what is happening despite the problems and struggles of the world around you.

It is God's pleasure to reveal things that He has hidden for us to discover. There is joy to be had in discovery. There is discovery in the waiting. Are you looking for it?

> *But there is nothing covered up that will not be revealed, neither hid that will not be known.* (Luke 12:2, KJV)

When you finally give everything up to God and not withhold anything from Him, you will discover the supernatural things that He is working around you. He will call you to do things that you didn't think you could do before. Some of these things are not exactly suggestions, they are commands. If God commands His people to do something then are we not to do them, despite how crazy that command might sound? Gideon may not have been confident about marching around the walls of Jericho but he did it in obedience to what God commanded. Think of it this way; when God gave the Ten Commandments the people didn't say, "Well, let's pray on it and see if we should move forward with these..." No! They simply obeyed. If God gives you a command in what you should do to advance His kingdom it is right to obey and not be idle in the waiting. God might be waiting too. He might be wondering if you will be obedient to the things He has called you to, rather than waiting for Him to move mountains before you even get your hands dirty. While we wait, God is still working. He doesn't need eight hours of sleep to be refreshed. If God works in the waiting perhaps, we also can work in the waiting.

Father God, give me the confidence and willingness to do everything and I mean everything You command of us in the waiting. I am looking for Your heart God, not my own in all that I do and say. Help me to recognize first Your commands of me as Your dearly loved child in scripture and in Your direct communication with me. I want to follow and obey so that I may see more of Your supernatural wonders and miracles that You would be glorified in ALL things. May my obedience result in others seeing Your love and mercy and lifting up Your name in Christ Jesus.

DAY 11

Filled With the Holy Spirit

What is the evidence of Holy Spirit within you?

Is it not our pleasure and our duty to obey and give God what is His? Our entire life is His. Is it not our good pleasure to want to show Him affection and love in every possible way we can?

As parents, aunts/uncles, or even grandparents when children ask us to do something like put on an animal mask, or crawl through a tiny space that you can barely fit in, there we are doing it. Was there ever a time in your life when you were trying to impress someone you liked and did things that were humiliating to gain their favor or at the very least be seen by them?

My children want me to wear this ridiculous costume because we absolutely need to win the family costume contest at school, and yes, I do it! Why? Why are we so willing to make a fool of ourselves for those that we have brought up or given life to? Because we are showing them another level of our love and affection. Why do we spend money on outfits and toys for our pets? Because we love them. God deserves that level of love and so much more!

When you spend your time with God, there's no tangible way to hug or kiss Him. There's only so many words of adoration you can convey and give without exhausting your earthly ability. God wants your affection just as you want His. If it is our good pleasure to show Him a greater level of love, why not find ways of doing that? Indeed, there is a way. What is the evidence of the Spirit living within you?

> *[17] These miraculous signs will accompany those who believe: They will cast out demons in my name, and they will speak in new languages. [18] They will be able to handle snakes with safety, and if they drink anything poisonous, it won't hurt them. They will be able to place their hands on the sick, and they will be healed.*
> Mark 16:17-18 (NLT)

And they were all filled with the Holy Ghost, and began to speak with other tongues, as the Spirit gave them utterance. (Acts 2:4, KJV) Raising the dead, healing the sick? Yes, these things please God! This is His love language! Obedience to Him looks like these things. We are so willing to look silly for those we love. We are ready to do an embarrassing song and dance for our friends or to take a dare. Why not for God? The Spirit will give you the ability through Christ but you must be the one to exercise it.

Lord, I know that I can be so caught up with what man thinks of me, and less attune with what You ask of me. May I be more mindful and more willing, and braver in showing You my love and affection for You in the way that You call me to. I pray that I set You as a seal upon my heart, as a seal upon my arm: for love IS stronger than death. I will proclaim Your name to all. I will allow myself to speak in tongues. I will pray to raise people to life again, and I will pray healing over the sick in Jesus's name. Continue to have favor on me Lord as I aim to grow closer and closer to You and to do what pleases You God, in Christ Jesus.

DAY 12

The Fruit of the Spirit

A discussion of the Holy Spirit would not be complete without talking about the Fruit of the Spirit. Fruit of the spirit is evidence that Holy Spirit is leading you. All of the aspects work together in harmony so that you conduct yourself the way Jesus would want you to. Each one is important on their own; however, it's hard to not have one fruit of the spirit without having another at the same time. For example, it is hard to not have peace when you have self-control. Or it is hard not to have love when you are showing kindness. Each one does need to be worked on although having all of them not only achieves the glorification of God but also protects you from doing something that would grieve the Holy Spirit or lead to disobedience. We will spend some time discussing the Holy Spirit in the next few days.

[22] *But the fruit of the Spirit is love, joy, peace, forbearance, kindness, goodness, faithfulness,* [23] *gen-*

tleness and self-control. Against such things there is no law. (Galatians 5:22-23, NIV)

While waiting for an answer, God can teach you the ways in which the Holy Spirit's fruits can help and support you. They will edify you in a time of need. They help you and equally as important, they help others.

Can we entertain the idea that God can do even better than that? When your heart is primed and ready to see God's goodness, it surely gets revealed. What if God's blessing to you in the waiting is not just to have you acquire these fruits of the spirit yourself during your time of trouble? Can you dig deep and think of how love, joy, peace, patience, kindness, goodness, faithfulness, gentleness, and/or self-control was given to you recently? Let's start there and see God and His miraculous timing, grace and mercy at work. He will sustain you. You just have to look harder and recognize it. This recognition and correct attribute of God will help give you the comfort you need in trying times.

Lord, I pray and commit that I will look for the good, not just in You, God, but in all others around me during my trials. I look for the fruit of the spirit that shines through from others so that I can be thankful and hopeful while I wait on You. I confess in the times where I was so downtrodden that I could only see my problems and it was difficult, but not impossible, to see the good You have worked out in my life. Even now in this moment, I will focus on what is going right and what fruit is being shared with me so that I may please You Father. I ask for Your revelation in finding all the good fruit that I may gather to sustain me during this time. I thank You for all the extra fruit that I can gather that spill off from others You have sent my way to share and comfort me. I will continue in this posture to please You, Father. I thank You in Jesus's name.

DAY 13

Love

There is no fear in love; but perfect love casts out fear, because fear involves punishment, and the one who fears is not perfected in love. (1 John 4:18, CSB)

We shouldn't be afraid in the waiting if we focus on God's love. We should never fear when we serve such a big God.

> *Better is a dish of vegetables where love is than a fattened ox served with hatred.* (Proverbs 15:17, NASB)

When we do acts of love, we have to have the right heart in doing it. We want to continue to do things in love despite our own circumstances. Sometimes, that looks like letting someone ahead of you in line even though you're also in a hurry. Sometimes it means having more patience with someone who just isn't understanding what you're saying. Sometimes, it is apologizing even when you don't feel like it. We can show love with actions, but it is far better to love well and have the right intention and reason to do so. We would also want that from God and from others.

Can you think of a time when someone has loved you well? Perhaps when you didn't deserve it? I recall one specific time that comes to mind for me of seeing an image of Jesus on the crucifix. We didn't deserve His perfect love but we still got it. Can you treasure that in your heart constantly so that when it comes time to love someone else well, you can remember the grace and mercy Jesus gave you so that your own act of showing love to others is true and genuine? That is why it is so important to have a loving mindset. To remember what we don't deserve when it comes to giving and showing love to other people. When we are hurt, or anxious or afraid, we forget how to love well. It becomes a selfish focus because your need is so great. God understands this, but He also wants to remind you that with Him we can overcome every obstacle and that it is right to show others love despite our own circumstances. That is how HE loves.

Might I also bring up the fact that Jesus shows compassion prior to doing a loving act such as healing, or opening blind eyes to see. We need love and compassion for our prayers to be effective. Otherwise, it is just lip service. Love people well and you will have compassion for them. When you have compassion and you lift them up in prayer God will move.

Father, I thank You for the way You love me. I thank You that Your love is perfect. That it doesn't hold back and that it is unconditional despite my own thoughts and actions toward You and Your people. Help me to show and convey love to others the way that is acceptable and pleasing to You. I want to love others well despite my own pain, situation or problem. I look forward to growing closer to Holy Spirit as You guide me in how to love. Be near to me, and speak to me Lord, in Jesus's name I pray.

DAY 14

Joy

The king shall joy in thy strength, O LORD; and in thy salvation how greatly shall he rejoice! (Psalms 21:1, KJV)

Behold, this is the joy of his way, and out of the earth shall others grow. (Job 8:19, KJV)

Things grow when joy is present. I was born from Joy, literally, that is my mother's name. I only realized recently how appropriate this prophetic occurrence was for me when God kept revealing to me that I was created to be a champion of joy. There were so many moments where my joy could have been stolen from me. I won't lie when I tell you that I didn't grow up with a charmed life. I grew up in what those in southern California might consider the ghetto. I knew that we didn't have much, but I didn't see how lowly we were because there was always food in the house and there was always laughter and joy amidst my family.

My family knew what it was to live with little and be happy. Paper decorations for Christmas because we couldn't afford to buy nice ornaments. Rice every day to fill our bellies when there weren't many choices and clean soft pillows despite sleeping on the floor many nights when cousins were staying over.

My grandmother moved from a third world country to come here and live the American Dream. Her children had every opportunity to get a great education, good jobs and they were proud and honored to serve in the US military. They saw their lives in the past and knew they had done better for their children. What a blessing in knowing that God would provide through the work of our hands. What a wonderful feeling of accomplishment. Joy really came in the mornings for us as a family. Waking up next to all of my cousins as we slept on the floor side by side and laughing and playing with anything, and everything, we could find to entertain us. We didn't care that we had very little space to ourselves with five brothers and their wives and children under the same roof. In fact, I didn't have a room of my own until I moved out of the house as an adult.

Very little space to be had but we were joyful. You can say we were taught and we modeled how to experience joy in every circumstance. It takes a certain level of discipline, resilience and grit to have joy in every circumstance.

Father, forgive me if even a moment goes by where I don't recognize how wonderful You have made my life. Just the comfort of a bed to sleep on or a full belly is enough to have joy and gladness. How easy I can forget Your blessings. May I always have that at the top of my mind and also spilling over. I pray others will see my joy and recognize that all of this comes only because of You, Lord Jesus. Bring joy into my life that I may share it with others and I rejoice and wait on You always. Thank You, Father!

DAY 15

Peace

If possible, so far as it depends on you, be at peace with all men. (Romans 12:18, NASB)

One of the titles that Jesus has is Prince of Peace. During a time when Rome was occupying Israel the Jewish people believed they would have a king that would rise up and fight against their oppressors of the day. How different for the people to recognize that Jesus came to bring their hearts peace, and to save them not from Romans by means of force but to save them from their sins.

Only when we accept Jesus into our hearts and are filled with the Holy Spirit can we truly experience that peace that surpasses all understanding. We have to let God in so that we might have peace within ourselves.

I used to have anxiety. As a child, I would be afraid that I would get locked out of the house, or that no one would come and pick me up from elementary school, or that there would not be enough food for everyone. The last thing caused me to have an unhealthy relationship with food and at ten years old and only three feet tall I managed to become triple digits on the scale. A battle that I didn't conquer until I was an adult.

Once I understood the nature of God and was truly baptized with the Holy Spirit, those anxieties slowly moved farther and farther into the background of my life. Then when I decided to not just accept Jesus into my heart but follow Him (in His ways) all of the strongholds of anxiety and stress about the things I couldn't control were demolished within me. I was truly set free. Then, and only then, did I experience true peace in my life. Only with God. Even relationships that were toxic and stressful, God made a way to distance me from those people and situations. Only He could orchestrate such a well-designed path for a life of peace. He did it for me and He can certainly do it for you.

> *13 Therefore put on the full armor of God, so that when the day of evil comes, you may be able to stand your ground, and after you have done everything, to stand. 14 Stand firm then, with the belt of truth buckled around your waist, with the breastplate of righteousness in place, 15 and with your feet fitted with the readiness that comes from the gospel of peace.*
>
> Ephesians 6:13-15 (NIV)

God You ARE the prince of peace. You are my deliverer and the one who brings me to a place of perfect peace in my heart when I am alone in Your presence. Continuously stay beside me, Holy Spirit, so that the peace of God will remain on me and can be felt by those in my proximity. That Your peace would flood me within to overflowing so that I may be able to spread Your peace to those people I encounter day in and day out. Thank You for always providing peace when everything around me might be out of sorts and out of order. Help me to truly walk with the armor of God that I may be fitted with the feet of peace wherever I go every day. Make me a worthy vessel to do Your work of peace in Jesus Christ. Amen.

DAY 16

Patience

I don't know about you but my patience tends to wear thin when my kids are nearing the end of their summer vacation. With them home all day there are just more opportunities to yell at, I mean correct, them. After a long day at work, the last thing you want to see are piles of toys, games, Legos, and whatnot all over the house. And all the dirty dishes spread throughout every available surface. Of course, they have the expectation that I will be the one to "help" clean up.

My first instinct is to gather my children so I can collectively reprimand them for all the random piles of stuff left out. Losing my temper with my kids is something I actively have to work on. I would like to think I have become better at correction without a blow up on my end. Although in hindsight, it's likely a combination of them growing less messy and being more mindful of responsibility. I'm still working on the patience part.

How many times do we leave our spiritual mess and dirty dishes for God to clean up? As our Father, we fully expect it of Him too, as we continuously act like the children that we are to Him. Thank God for His patience with us. Can you imagine if He blew up on us for not cleaning up after ourselves? I tell you what, the thought of a Job sized whirlwind of God's power is not something I would ever want to experience. Job had to gird up his loins and he was actually a righteous man of God. Can we humble ourselves to recognize we don't deserve the patience God gives us? Even better than His most obedient servant Job? And, by the way, what did I do in my life to even deserve that level of patience He gives me?

Then the LORD answered Job from the whirlwind. He said:

> ² *Who is this who obscures My counsel with ignorant words?* ³ *Get ready to answer Me like a man; when I question you, you will inform Me.* ⁴ *Where were you when I established the earth? Tell Me, if you have understanding.* ⁵ *Who fixed its dimensions? Certainly you know! ho stretched a measuring line across it?* ⁶ *What supports its foundations? r who laid its cornerstone* ⁷ *while the morning stars sang together nd all the sons of God shouted for joy?*
> Job 38:1-7 (NIV)

No, thank you, I prefer God's patience... May we always remember God's kindness when we have moments with others that deserve that level of patience in dealing with us and the situation we are waiting in. Let's pray!

Father, You are so patient I can't even bend my brain enough to understand it! I do receive the patience You bestow on me regularly and I pray that I am mindful of that when I am called to be patient in my own situation and in my own life. Will You help me remember that patience is something that pleases You? I will try harder to show patience in every circumstance as I wait on You Lord, as I know Your strength will sustain me while I wait. I pray in Jesus. Amen.

DAY 17

Kindness

One thing I have struggled with, and have slowly come to the realization of, is that we tend to connect negative attributes to God. When something is hard and you can't seem to overcome the situation on your own, there's a tendency to wonder why God allows for that situation or that struggle. Some people, especially those who are new in Christ, may incorrectly believe that the negative circumstance they are in is God's doing. So often I have heard people of little faith or no faith at all say things like, "Why did God do that to me?" "Why is God punishing me?" and other similar quips. The reason people incorrectly identify these bad traits with God, is because they are not close to Him.

I saw God's kindness one day when I was at the LA County courthouse. I got to hear other people's arraignments and testimonies to plead their case in court.

One particular man was charged with crossing the intersection where there is a camera that will take your photo if you cross the intersection while the light is red.

The man testified that he didn't run a red light and that his tires merely stopped on the line and in good faith in the appropriate place. Because his tires were crossing the line the camera was prompted to take a picture and he received a ticket. The judge tried to be lenient, but decided he was too far into the intersection and they still found him guilty. The man said "I don't believe I should be punished for this." to which the judge replied "I'm not in the business of punishment, but I am in the business of upholding the law to make sure you and everyone else is safe."

    I am guilty of having the feeling about that judge being a gavel smashing punisher and attributing that feeling to God. For many years, I have learned to see God's kindness and His just ways of mercy to protect me. Not to punish me. When we are still caught up in our own broken ways we can't see the kindness in God for what it is. Can we take a minute to see from a kingdom perspective (as mysterious as it is) and look at why God might do what He does? Look at God from a perspective where we understand that He is ever trying to protect and help us. He is not the bad guy. Now that I clearly see and understand that through the power of the Holy Spirit dwelling within me, I feel righteous anger when someone thinks God is responsible for something terrible or bad happening in their lives.

I pray you would also come to the realization that God is FOR you, NOT against you.

> *What, then, shall we say in response to these things? If God is for us, who can be against us?*
> (Romans 8:31, NIV)

You are incredibly kind to us Lord, even when we misrepresent You. I pray that I would seek You out and recognize when it is God and when it is not; when it is my own flesh or others causing the sinful ways that lead to negative things that happen in life and when it is You trying to shield and protect me from my own and other's free will. I pray for Your kindness as I continue on this journey of growing closer to You and understanding Your nature. May I always focus on Your kindness in every circumstance. Holy Spirit continue to help in renewing my mind each day to reflect on His kindness that I don't deserve but have. In Christ Jesus alone. Amen.

DAY 18

Goodness

When I was young, in my very early twenties I lost my father. He died in a motorcycle accident. An unexpected death can be truly painful. You don't get a chance to say goodbye or prepare in any way. As God says, life is but a vapor.

Raised by the village; my cousins were really more my siblings. My dad had eight brothers and the younger five brothers collectively took care of each other and their children as we were one big family. When he died, I had four uncles step up and continue to care for me like I was their own. What person can say they had several father figures that cared for them? So much so and in such a way that I never lost a father figure in my life. Six months after my dad died, I lost one other uncle to suicide. But God, in His omniscience knew I would come to rely on another uncle, and another, and another. Yet another uncle became estranged due to his choices in life and I lost his care and counsel during some critical years, and God raised yet another uncle/father for me. It sounds crazy but I can see the fingerprints of His goodness in this chain of events. Even when life was dark and I could choose to play the victim, I now can reflect and see instead how good God was to me. Where in the natural it might seem tragedy after tragedy, the true goodness of God is seen in the favor He has had over my life all these years in the midst of chaos.

> *The Lord is compassionate and gracious, slow to anger, abounding in love. He relents from sending calamity.* (Psalms 103:8, NIV)

How shall I return this goodness of God? Or better yet, how can I steward the goodness of God in my life? In the waiting and healing there is mercy and love if we would only come to recognize it. I pray this day that you would reflect on His love and mercy for you. I choose to pass on the goodness that God has shown me to others. Once recognized, we can't go on without sharing that same goodness to others. Something that seems so disparaging can be changed in an instant when someone shows you a small kindness. When you are forgiven for a wrong you have done, or if an officer lets you off with a warning, or if someone allows you into a venue despite you being late it can change the atmosphere. There are so many instances where God shows you His goodness through others. Let's continue to keep those reminders within us so that when a wrong is done, we are quick to show goodness in return. What spills over when you are hurt or wronged should be kind and loving when you are filled with the goodness of God. That is what should be on the surface.

God, how can I be obedient and bless You as You have blessed me with Your goodness? Reveal to me how I can show goodness to others this day and every day of my life. Would You fill me up so much to overflowing that only Your goodness would spill out through me when I hit those bumps in the road. I want to be so filled with the things of You, God, so that in my waiting others can bear to be around me. I want to be so filled with Holy Spirit that You inspire my actions. Your goodness cannot be matched and for that I cannot express my gratitude. In Your good and precious name. Amen.

DAY 19

Faithfulness

When I get around to writing another book it would be about the testimony of the numerous times that God has saved me again and again. I can go back and think on all of the good things that have happened, all of the moments when God showed up, and all of the times He saved me from a situation and even from myself.

The fact that I can reflect on those moments and find God shows God's faithfulness. He is faithful to seek us out again and again. We, like the Israelites, might be going down the path of righteousness but we are also susceptible to falling into bad habits and patterns that are not good for us when we forget to keep our focus on God. He continues to seek us out.

> [4] *"Suppose one of you has a hundred sheep and loses one of them. Doesn't he leave the ninety-nine in the open country and go after the lost sheep until he finds it?* [5] *And when he finds it, he joyfully puts it on his shoulders* [6] *and goes home. Then he calls his friends and neighbors together and says, 'Rejoice*

with me; I have found my lost sheep.' ⁷ I tell you that in the same way there will be more rejoicing in heaven over one sinner who repents than over ninety-nine righteous persons who do not need to repent.

Luke 15:1-7 (NIV)

When we allow Jesus to be our shepherd there is no length He won't go to seek us out. When we recognize that through allowing Holy Spirit to live within us, we also can have faithfulness in all things. We recognize God's faithfulness to us and in being aware of that we are able to be faithful in our lives. I urge you to practice recalling and also writing down all of the moments you remember God showing His faithfulness in your life. Take time to think of people and situations that God has brought into your life in an act of faithfulness to you. Be thankful for those times. When we can recall the Father's faithfulness and come from a posture of grateful hearts and minds, we are able to act in faithfulness for God. We can do His will which requires that we are faithful in all things too.

Father, I lift up all those who have had difficulty in seeing the evidence of Your faithfulness in their lives. I begin with interceding for others and for myself that I would be reminded of all the good and faithful acts You have done on my be-

half if only to gain my heart. I thank You, Father, for all the moments you have saved me. For all the moments You have shown me mercy when I didn't deserve it. For all the moments that You have blessed me unnecessarily. It is Your true faithfulness to me that allows me to show faithfulness in doing the work You have called me to. May I always abide and tarry on the faithfulness You continue to shower me with especially in the waiting. In Your most holy name. Amen.

DAY 20

Gentleness

If anyone is caught in a trespass, you who are spiritual restore such a one in a spirit of gentleness (Galatians 6:1, BLB)

The very definition of gentleness is stated as the softness of an action or effect. When we are gentle, we shouldn't confuse that with being weak. Just because your motions are soft doesn't make you soft. We, who are in Christ, have the ability to do what Jesus says we will do. As true disciples of Jesus, we have to know and recognize His power and authority within us; which is by no means weak. It is the opposite. When you understand your own strength but can still control the manner of which you yield it, that is gentleness.

Gentleness is such an important and significant skill in life. Imagine a toddler who just picked up something heavy (like a rock). Your first instinct is to immediately get that heavy object out of their hands. Why? Because toddlers love to experiment with the laws of gravity. Potentially they can either throw the heavy object or drop it. Gentleness is not something that comes innately to us as human beings, it is taught. Another example is in teaching young children how to pet an animal. Little kids don't always understand how strong they are, and they are curiously strong, so they need to be taught not to squeeze, push or put all of their weight down on a dog/cat or other creatures. You often hear someone say "gently" or "nice" if you've ever been to a petting zoo.

Consider your actions the next time you find yourself speaking with another person that might need some correction or direction or help. Are we verbally pummeling them with the power and strength within us, or are we exercising restraint? When we can restrain or guide that power (either in speech or physically) we are showing gentleness. The best way to harness that power is to ask Holy Spirit to guide your actions, words and even thoughts. Why is this important? It could be the difference between turning someone's heart toward or away from God. We absolutely need gentleness, especially in times of waiting. We absolutely need to exercise the same gentleness with others despite our circumstances.

> *For the kingdom of God does not consist in talk but in power. What do you wish? Shall I come to you with a rod, or with love in a spirit of gentleness?* (1 Corinthians 4:20-21, ESV)

Father in heaven, may I always have gentleness in my mind when speaking and interacting with others. Show me and guide me in Your gentleness so that I may better understand it and appropriately convey gentleness with others who are in need. Help me, Father, to focus more on how to communicate with gentleness to others, rather than being distracted by what I'm trying to do or say. I look for Your favor in all that I do and that I may seek opportunities to testify of Your gentleness and goodness toward me. May I glorify Your name above all else and share You with others with the gentleness that You have planted within me. I pray all of this in Jesus's name. Amen.

DAY 21

Self-Control

What exactly is self-control? It's curious that self-control is the last fruit of the spirit that is listed in Galatians 5:22. The definition of self-control according to *Webster's Dictionary* is, "restraint exercised over one's own impulses, emotions, or desires."

My idea of self-control brings everything full circle in terms of what God is seeking us to gain in being filled with the Holy Spirit. I like to think of it this way; self-control means not losing your love, joy, peace, patience, kindness, goodness, gentleness, or faithfulness. If we have these virtues at the top of mind, we will be in more control of what God is asking and shaping us to be.

Could we extend that idea out further and say that self-control is also in our demeanor, how we express ourselves and how we appear outwardly to others when we interact with them? Are we expressing a demeanor that shows we can control feelings and actions even in the toughest times? Can we be all of these manifestations of the Spirit and not lose our cool the moment something goes wrong? Can we be these fruits to our own selves? Do we see ourselves the way God sees us? If we did, people probably wouldn't struggle with things like depression, anxiety, or self-consciousness. It sounds simple, but God wouldn't highlight this as fruit of the Spirit if we could do it in our own power. Having Holy Spirit within us is the only way to gain these fruits in our life. Fruit is what is birthed from allowing God to plant these seeds within us, to let those seeds grow and bear fruit. That doesn't come by dismissing Him or passively having God in our lives when it benefits us.

Can we make a commitment (which requires self-control) to allow the Spirit to live within us, and abide in Him as well so that these seeds will grow? As we talked about early on in these devotionals, the waiting period, if we allow God to work through all of our hardest situations, will reveal true character. The goal is not to continue a path of human nature but to adopt and really receive the true divine nature which is our gift of receiving Jesus in our lives. We should grow in the fruit He provides and the yearning to want to be the person God is calling us to become. Let's not squander the time we have in moments of waiting, but instead allow for self-control to guide and shape us to a greater purpose and kingdom desires. If we do not grow in times of distress, we have wasted an opportunity to exercise self-control and all other fruits of the Spirit for His glory and His purpose.

> *Through these he has given us his very great and precious promises, so that through them you may participate in the divine nature, having escaped the corruption in the world caused by evil desires.*
> (2 Peter 1:4, NIV)

LORD and master of my life, as I continue to wait on You, I ask that You create in me a pure heart, with pure desires, and Godly motives. Help me to have self-control in all that I do, from my actions toward others, to what comes out of my mouth, and, in fact, even what goes in. I want to be a clean-living temple for Holy Spirit to dwell in every aspect of my life; physically, emotionally, and mentally. I know that life will go well for me if only I can obey You always. I want what You want, God. I desire what You desire. In Jesus's name. Amen.